D0593492

POCKET PRAYERS FOR PEACE AND JUSTICE

Pocket Prayers for Peace and Justice

COMPILED BY
Christian Aid

WITH AN INTRODUCTION
BY Bishop Joe Aldred

CHURCH HOUSE
PUBLISHING

Church House Publishing
Church House
Great Smith Street
London SW1P 3NZ
Tel: 020 7898 1451
Fax: 020 7898 1449

ISBN 0 7151 4021 3

Published 2004 by Church House Publishing

Typeset by Vitaset, Paddock Wood, Kent
Printed in England by the University Printing House,
Cambridge

CONTENTS

INTRODUCTION

One of the privileges of our God-centred humanity is to converse with God, the Creator and Sustainer of all things. I recall hearing the great 'prayer warriors', among whom I have been blessed to be raised, prefacing their prayers dramatically with the words of the song, ''Tis the blessed hour of prayer, when our hearts lowly bend, and we gather to Jesus our Saviour and friend; when we come to Him in faith, His protection to share, what a balm for the weary, oh how sweet to be there'. However, it is even more blessed to discover that we do not have to wait for special times to pray: God is ready for a conversation with us at any time and place. This *Pocket Prayers for Peace and Justice* provides us with an excellent resource for maintaining a prayerful lifestyle. Its focus on prayers dealing with the nature of God, peace, justice and good news for the poor ensures that our prayerful attention is focused on many of life's perplexing issues that ask searching questions of our human existence as individuals and groups. Prayer, though, is much more than words. And so these written prayers must come off the pages and become incarnational in such a way that we are driven to act also!
Joe Aldred

Dr Aldred is an ordained bishop in the Church of God of Prophecy, a worldwide Pentecostal church. He is currently Associate Pastor at Cannon Street Memorial Baptist Church, London, and the Secretary for Minority Ethnic Christian Affairs, Churches Together in Britain and Ireland.

*

GOD OF PEACE AND GOD OF JUSTICE

*I will feed [my sheep] with justice ... I will make
with them a covenant of peace.*

Ezekiel 34.16, 25

*Justice and peace are part of the nature of God
himself and part of his purpose for his people.
So before we come to pray specifically for peace
and justice in God's world and in our lives, the
prayers that open this collection focus on God
and our response to him and to his Son.*

*

A call to worship

Hear the invitation of the prophet Isaiah:
Come, let us go up to God's
holy mountain,
that we may learn to walk
in all God's ways.
For God will judge between the nations,
and shall decide for many peoples.
And they shall beat their swords
into ploughshares,
And their spears into pruning hooks.
Nation shall not lift up sword
against nation,
neither shall they learn war any more.
Let us come before God and learn
God's ways of peace.

cf Isaiah 2.1-4
Ruth Duck

✳

A prayer based on the 23rd Psalm

The Lord is my shepherd;
I have everything I need.
He lets me see a country of justice and peace
and directs my steps towards this land.
He gives me power.
He guides me in the paths of victory,
as he has promised.
Even if a full-scale violent confrontation
     breaks out
I will not be afraid, Lord,
for you are with me.
Your shepherd's power and love protect me.
You prepared for me my freedom,
where all my enemies can see it;
you welcome me as an honoured guest
and fill my cup with righteousness
     and peace.
I know that your goodness and love will
     be with me all my life
and your liberating love will be my home
as long as I live.

Pastor Kameeta from Namibia

An Advent prayer

Let us rejoice and be glad
  for the Lord God is near:
he is coming in power to save his people.
Lord Jesus, we pray that your coming
may transform our work;
help us to work eagerly and honestly,
to know that everything we do
has a place in your purpose.
Through our lives and by our prayer,
  your Kingdom come.

We pray that your coming
may transform our family life:
may we learn in our homes the peace,
love and generosity
we should show to all people.
Through our lives and by our prayer,
  your Kingdom come.

We pray that your coming
  may transform society:
inspire us to hunger and thirst
  for what is right,
to work against injustice
  wherever we find it.
Through our lives and by our prayer,
  your Kingdom come.

We pray that your coming
    may transform the world,
bringing peace and justice to all nations,
    and turning
the forces of science and technology
    to good ends.
**Through our lives and by our prayer,
    your Kingdom come.**

Pax Christi

A meditation on the incarnation

Reader 1: The Word for our sake became
poverty, clothed as the poor ...

Reader 2: And the Word blew its spirit over
the dry bones of the churches ...

Reader 3: The Word, a clarion horn,
woke us up from the lethargy
that had robbed us of our Hope ...

Reader 1: The Word became a path
in the jungle,
a decision in the fields,
unity among ordinary people
and a star for those few
who sow dreams.

Reader 2: Tired knees were strengthened,
trembling hands were stilled,
and the people who wandered
in darkness saw the light!

Reader 3: The Word makes justice rain
and peace come forth
from the furrows in the land.

1, 2 & 3: The Lord be with you.

All: **And also with you.**
May God's kingdom come:
God's will be done,
on earth
as in heaven.
Amen.

Adapted by R. Dudley from Julia Esquivel, Those who saw the star

Beatitudes

Blessed are those whose spirit
    has been shaped by poverty;
for theirs is the Kingdom of heaven.

Blessed are those who are sick at heart
    to see power abused;
for they shall be invited to the feast.

Blessed are those who are not arrogant;
for they shall inherit the earth.

Blessed are those who are desperate
    for justice;
for they shall eat and drink their fill.

Blessed are the compassionate;
for they shall have compassion shown
    to them when they need it.

Blessed are those who refuse to be corrupted;
for they shall not be afraid to come
    face to face with God.

Blessed are those who take action
    to bring about peace;
for they shall truly be called God's own.

Blessed are those who carry wounds
    suffered in the struggle for justice;
for theirs is the Kingdom of heaven.

Christian Aid

A prayer based on The Lord's Prayer

Our Father who is in us here on earth,
holy is your name in the hungry
    who share their bread and their song.

Your kingdom come,
a generous land where confidence
    and truth reign.

Let us do your will,
bring a cool breeze for those who sweat.

You are giving us our daily bread
when we manage to get back our lands
    or to get a fairer wage.

Forgive us
for keeping silent in the face of injustice
    and for burying our dreams.

Don't let us fall into the temptation of
    taking up the same arms as the enemy,
but deliver us from evil which disunites us.

And we shall have believed in humanity
    and in life,
and we shall have known your kingdom
    which is being built for ever and ever.

From a poor community in Central America

Prayers of calling

Jesus calls us to journey with him,
to journey with him to a woman pouring
perfume in a house at Bethany,
to journey with him to a man pouring water,
    clearing up after the devastation of war,
to journey with him to a woman
        pouring lotion on the bruises
        of a husband's violence.

Jesus calls us to speak out with him,
to speak out for the beauty
        of a woman's extravagance,
to speak out for the unveiling of rules
        that deny people's existence,
to speak out for justice
        for the poorest of the poor.

And Jesus calls us to celebrate
        in the dance of liberation.
Jesus calls us to celebrate love
        wherever it is found.
Jesus calls us to celebrate the many gifts
        offered by women and men.
Jesus calls us to celebrate the dignity
        and worth of all people.

Clare McBeath

We are all of the Kingdom on earth.
   In all holiness we are called
   to share in creation.
   We are the branches of the vine.
We are of the Kingdom on earth.
   In all holiness we are called
   to share in its wealth, to allow people
   to grow crops to feed themselves.
   We are the branches of the vine.
We are of the Kingdom on earth.
   In all holiness we are called
   to create a just society which allows
   for the human dignity of all;
   that allows people life, food, freedom
   to walk in their own land.
   We are the branches of the vine.
We are called to reject the false gods
   of weaponry systems and economic
   systems that are killing people
   both of starvation and 'fall out'
   and violating the earth's resources.
   We are the branches of the vine.
We are of the Kingdom of heaven on earth.
   We are called to vulnerability,
   we are called to strength,
   we are called to laughter,
   we are called to tears,
   we are called to the depths of love.
   We are the branches of the vine.

Jenny Hunt

A prayer of invocation

Yours, O God, is the vineyard
    and its harvest,
yours the kingdom of justice and peace.
You call your people to tend its growth.
Bless the work entrusted to our hand,
that we may offer you an abundance
    of just works,
a rich harvest of peace.
We ask this through our Lord Jesus Christ,
    your Son,
who lives and reigns with you
    in the unity of the Holy Spirit,
    God for ever and ever.
Amen.

Julie M. Hulme

✳

A prayer for courage

Our God, we would see Jesus as
    the cherished babe lying on the hay,
    the energetic healer of Galilee,
    the triumphant risen Christ.
We confess that we find it troubling
    to speak of Jesus as the humble servant,
    calling us to take up a cross.
We hesitate when loyalty to Jesus
    means discomfort, inconvenience,
        suffering or death.
Forgive our too-easy affirmations;
    our noble Sunday-morning intentions
    which quickly slide into
        weekday compromises.
Nurture us in the eagerness of children,
    the boldness of prophets,
    the visions of poets,
    the courage of disciples.
May we continue to trust your promise
        of a time of peace,
    when swords will be beaten
        into ploughshares,
    when you will wipe away all tears,
    when pain and death will be no more.

May we give our lives in service
     to that vision,
   living with and for others
   as if the promise were already fulfilled.
Amen.

Kenneth L. Gibble

✳

A prayer for vision

Lord:
Help us to see in the groaning of creation
not death but birth pangs;
help us to see in suffering a promise
     for the future,
because it is a cry against the inhumanity
     of the present.
Help us to glimpse in protest
     the dawn of justice,
in the Cross the pathway to resurrection,
and in suffering the seeds of joy.

Rubem Alves

A prayer of praise

Glory be to you, O Holy God,
    you who are love and justice.
We praise you for the gifts you have made
    in creating the world
and human beings in your likeness.
We praise you for opening up for us
    a new way of life
    in Jesus Christ.
We praise you for calling us,
    through the Holy Spirit,
    to follow Jesus Christ
and to seek to bring justice for all.

Women's World Day of Prayer, 1990

*

A litany for peace and justice

Leader: O God, the heavens are yours
and the earth is yours.
All our life belongs to you.
**People: Make us your messengers
of peace and justice.**
May your kingdom come and your will
be done on earth, as it is in heaven.
**Make us your messengers of peace
and justice.**
May all injustice, violence, and oppression
give way to fairness, mercy
and good will.
**Make us your messengers of peace
and justice.**
Teach us to use the manifold resources
of the earth so that none may waste
and none may want.
**Make us your messengers of peace
and justice.**
In all our labours, may cooperation
triumph over conflict;
may all people find their reward
in work that serves the good of all.
**Make us your messengers of peace
and justice.**

Keep alive the holy fire within the hearts
    of all who dare to be the voices
    of unwelcome wisdom.
  Make us willing to hear hard demands.
**Make us your messengers of peace
    and justice.**
Fill us with a passion for righteousness
    and a zeal to serve where there is need.
  Fill us with a purpose that is holy
    and right and just.
  Help us to love the noblest and best.
**Make us your messengers of peace
    and justice.**
**All: Unto you, O God, be all might
    and majesty, Dominion and power,
    both now and evermore.**
Amen.

Walter Russell Bowie, Lift up your hearts (adapted)

Affirming the faith

Leader: We celebrate the resurrected Jesus,
     who lives among us,
People: whose Spirit empowers us
     to remove barriers,
   tear down walls, heal divisions,
   and seek shalom without and within.
We celebrate the resurrected Jesus,
     who lives among us,
whose Spirit empowers us
   to see our sister's good as our own,
   to be our brother's advocate,
   to love our neighbour as ourselves,
   and to contribute to the well-being
   of every part of Christ's body.
All: so that indeed we can build up,
     and grow up,
   and be joined together
     into a new structure:
   where Christ's Spirit dwells,
   where Christ's Spirit empowers us
   to be shalom-seekers, shalom-finders,
     and shalom-makers!

From Words for Worship

PRAYING FOR PEACE

Peace I leave with you; my peace I give to you.
                                              John 14.27

*In praying for peace we recognize our inability
to establish peace in our own strength. We need
God's help to find and maintain peace in our
personal relationships and in and between the
communities to which we belong. Because
Jesus' gift of peace is not simply the absence
of conflict. It is constructive and dynamic,
challenging and changing our relationships
with one another and with God.*

Personal peace with God

O Lord my God,
grant us your peace;
already, indeed, you have made us rich
    in all things!
Give us that peace of being at rest,
that Sabbath peace,
the peace which knows no end.

St Augustine, Confessions XIII

Risen Christ,
Your voice makes itself heard
Peacefully in the Gospel.
You say to us:
Do not be worried.
Only one thing is needed –
A heart which listens to my Word
And to the Holy Spirit.
Amen.

Brother Roger of Taizé

Do not smile and say
you are already with us.
Millions do not know you
and to us who do
what is the difference:
what is the point of your presence
if our lives do not alter?
Change our lives.
Shatter our complacency.
Make your word
flesh of our flesh,
blood of our blood
and our life's purpose.
Take away the quietness
of a clear conscience.
Press us uncomfortably,
for only thus
that other peace is made,
your peace.

Dom Helder Camara in The Desert is Fertile

Preparation for worship

As God's people, we have gathered.
We may be discouraged,
    dismayed, discordant with life.
Let us sit together,
    sharing the solace of silence.
Let us possess the peace of God's presence.
    And be wrapped in the warmth
        of God's love.
Let us be comforted and quieted,
    prepared for communion with God
    and fellowship with one another.

From Words for Worship

*

A prayer of invocation

O God,
we praise you in our worship today
    that Mary responded to your Spirit
    and was your servant to bring salvation.
Let us give ourselves also, as your servants;
    let us be bearers of good news
    and messengers of mercy and peace,
    through Christ we pray.
Amen.

From Words for Worship

A prayer at Christmas

Child of Bethlehem
house of bread;
Man of Jerusalem
city of peace:
You have loved us
without limit or condition;
in our greatness and in our misery,
in our folly and in our virtue:
May your hand be always upon us
and may your heart be within us
so that we too
may become bread and peace for
    one another.

John Hammond OSB

A prayer for compassion

God, my Lord.
I believe that you are present everywhere.
I believe that your presence is specially
found among the poor, the needy,
the fatherless or motherless orphans
and the sick.
By working for social justice, freedom,
peace and unity, I know that I am
working with you for your kingdom.
But with all this awareness I still fail to find
you among the poor and the needy
and hence I fail to bring about peace,
unity and justice.
I still crave for power and position.
I crave for all the comforts
which the world can give.
I love wealth.
I love security.
Help me, Lord, to realize the needs
of those down-trodden.
Help me, Lord, to strive
for the betterment of my brethren.
Help me to be a man for others.
Otherwise, give me the courage to say
that I am not a Christian any more.
Amen.

Prayer of an Indian Christian

Before falling asleep

O Lord, grant that this night
we may sleep in peace.
And that in the morning
our awakening may be also in peace.
May our daytime
be cloaked in your peace.
Protect us and inspire us
to think and act only out of love.
Keep far from us all evil;
may our paths be free from all obstacles
from where we go out
until the time we return home.

Babylonian Talmud

Peace in relationships

A prayer for Church unity

Lord Jesus Christ,
who said to your apostles,
'Peace I leave with you,
    my peace I give to you';
look not on our sins
    but on the faith of your Church
and grant it the peace and unity
    of your kingdom;
where you are alive and reign
    with the Father
in the unity of the Holy Spirit,
one God, now and for ever.
Amen.

Common Worship

A prayer for peace
in difficult circumstances

Mother me, my Father,
that I may step unbowed
from safe within your haven
to face a hostile crowd.

Mother me, my Father,
and help to ease the pain
of taunts and tears and teasing
and make me love again.

Mother me, my Father,
with hands so deeply scarred,
that I may touch some other
whose suffering is hard.

Mother me, my Father,
that all my life be styled
on loving like a mother
and trusting like a child.

Helen McKinnon

A prayer of thanksgiving

O Lord:
in a world where many are lonely:
we thank you for our friendships.

In a world where many are captive:
we thank you for our freedom.

In a world where many are hungry:
we thank you for your provision.

We pray that you will:
enlarge our sympathy,
deepen our compassion,
and give us grateful hearts.

In Christ's name.

Terry Waite

✳

A prayer for personal understanding

O Lord, open my eyes
that I may see the need of others,
open my ears that I may hear their cries,
open my heart so that they may not be
    without succour.
Let me not be afraid to defend the weak
because of the anger of the strong,
nor afraid to defend the poor
because of the anger of the rich.
Show me where love and hope and faith
    are needed
and use me to bring them to these places.
Open my eyes and ears that I may,
    this coming day,
be able to do some work of peace for you.

Alan Paton

A prayer from Sudan

And though I behold a man hate me,
　I will love him.
　O God, Father, help me, Father!
　O God, Father, help me, Father!
And even though I behold a man hate me,
　I will love him.

Prayer of a dying man, Dinka, Sudan

✳

A prayer for others

Lord,
strengthen the hands of those who work
to draw together
people of different races.
May the children who play together
remain friendly
as they grow older.
May students enter deeply
into each other's worlds.
May those who live as neighbours
or work together
strive to create
truly human bonds.

Caryl Micklem

A prayer of commitment

God, we believe
      that you have called us together
to broaden our experience of you
      and of each other.
We believe that we have been called
to help in healing the many wounds
      of society
and in reconciling man to man
      and man to God.
Help us, as individuals or together,
to work, in love, for peace,
      and never to lose heart.
We commit ourselves to each other –
in joy and sorrow.
We commit ourselves to all who share
      our belief in reconciliation –
to support and stand by them.
We commit ourselves
      to the way of peace –
in thought and deed.
We commit ourselves to you –
as our guide and friend.

Corrymeela Community, Ireland

A prayer of longing

Leader: O for a world where everyone
respects each other's ways,
People: where love is lived and all is done
with justice and with praise.
O for a world where goods are shared
and misery relieved,
where truth is spoken, children spared,
equality achieved.
We welcome one world family
and struggle with each choice
that opens us to unity
and gives our vision voice.
The poor are rich, the weak are strong,
the foolish ones are wise.
Tell all who mourn, outcasts belong,
who perishes will rise.
All: O for a world preparing for
God's glorious reign of peace,
where time and tears will be no more,
and all but love will cease.

Miriam T. Winter, Womanword (adapted)

＊

Prayers to remove barriers

O God,
by your Son Jesus Christ,
you have broken down
the walls of partition
between Jew and Gentile, slave and free,
rich and poor, male and female.
Break down all the barriers that divide us;
remove all the hindrances
that keep us apart.
Reveal our jealousies
and show us our pride;
cure our alienation;
open up our narrowness.
Shatter all prejudice
though we may have different histories,
different cultures, different viewpoints.
May we live together as loving neighbours,
in honour preferring one another,
to the glory of your great name.
Amen.

From Words for Worship

God of all the centuries,
we long to see an end
    to the lines that divide:
the lines that scar families,
the lines that deface religions,
the lines that embattle nations.
May you, O God, who crossed the line
    between heaven and earth,
work a miracle in the hearts of humans
and in the destinies of all countries
    enduring civil war.
Amen.

Christian Aid/ Peter Graystone

❊

Peace in the world

For the Middle East

Pray not for Arab or Jew, for Palestinian
or Israeli, but pray rather for ourselves,
that we might not divide them in our
prayers, but keep them both together
in our hearts.

Based on a prayer of a Palestinian Christian

✳

A prayer for Sudan

Peace! How I long to hear you
come to our land.
Run, run, we are waiting for you,
our children are crying for you;
our mothers are praying for you.

Peace! How I long to see you
spread your light to my people,
bright like the morning sun.
Let your rays fall on my people,
my beautiful African people.

A prayer from the Adjumani district of Sudan

*

A prayer for courage and vision

O God, give us the courage
    to offer the hand of forgiveness
to those who have wronged us,
and the humility to serve
    all those in our communities
whose lives are still broken and lost.

We know that through the many hardships
    we have faced,
your love and presence have been constant.

O God, give us the vision to see you
    in our neighbour,
and the joy to celebrate our diversity
so that we may work together
    with all in this land
to build a peaceful future for our children.
Amen.

Carolyn Boyd

A prayer of repentance

Lord Jesus Christ,
    you are the way of peace.
Come into the brokenness
      of our lives and our land
    with your healing love.
Help us to bow before you
      in true repentance,
    and to bow to one another
      in true repentance.
By the fire of your Holy Spirit,
    melt our hard hearts
    and consume the pride and prejudice
      which separate us.
Fill us, O Lord, with your perfect love,
    which casts out our fear,
    and bind us together in that unity
    which you share with the Father
    and the Holy Spirit for ever.
Amen.

From Words for Worship

For those who live in places where there is no peace

We lift before you, Lord God, our brothers and sisters who seek to serve you faithfully in countries where government is tyrannical, corrupt or chaotic. We ask that you will strengthen them, encourage them, and show them what is right. We pray that we may learn from them to do what is best instead of what is easiest, and to do what is good even when we are fearful. In the name of Jesus, whose example we seek to follow. **Amen.**

Christian Aid/ Peter Graystone

*

God of holy peace,
　we are accustomed to the darkness
　　of our world,
　accustomed to tragedy, sorrow, worry.
Like the shepherds sitting
　　in the darkness, expecting nothing,
we are familiar with dim hope.
Yet we brood over our troubled lives
　　and wicked world,
wondering when you will come in power
to bring peace to all hearts and lands.
Break the grip of darkness;
let your peace dawn in our hearts!
Look with favour upon your people;
grant your blessing.
Should angels bring clear messages
　　for our lives,
let us with wonder accept your news
　　of love
as the generous gift it is.
Amen.

Diane Karay

Prayers for reconciliation

O God Eternal, good beyond all that is
good, fair beyond all that is fair,
in whom is calmness and peace:
Reconcile the differences which divide us
from one another and bring us back
into the unity of love which may bear
some likeness to your divine nature.
Grant that we may be spiritually one,
both within ourselves
and with one another,
through the grace, mercy and tenderness
of your Son, Jesus Christ.
Amen.

Your Will Be Done

Lord Jesus, your sign of reconciliation is
the Cross, in all its breadth and length and
height and depth. Teach us to share it with
you and our sisters and brothers so that
we may learn to act justly, to walk humbly,
to love tenderly. And so, waiting upon the
Spirit, become instruments of your peace,
to the glory of the Father.

The Hengrave Community Prayer, England

✳

Praying for peacemakers

Almighty God,
whose will is to restore all things
in your beloved Son, the king of all:
govern the hearts and minds
   of those in authority,
and bring the families of the nations,
divided and torn apart
   by the ravages of sin,
to be subject to his just and gentle rule;
who is alive and reigns with you
   and the Holy Spirit,
one God, now and for ever.
Amen.

Alternative Service Book 1980

✳

From the land of the resurrection
and the cradle of the promise of salvation
to all humankind through Jesus Christ
our Lord, and with a candle of hope,
we pray to you, God our Father,
that the action of peace-seekers
and peace-makers may bear fruit so that
hope will take the place of despair,
justice will prevail over oppression,
peace will turn strife into love.

Palestinian women, Jerusalem

✳

O Prince of Peace,
confound all those who seek
to change the world through violence;
prosper all those whose hearts
are set upon reconciliation;
and teach us, when confronted by evil,
how to respond with both the strength
and the sacrifice of Christ.
Amen.

Christian Aid/ Peter Graystone

O Christ, you are the light of the world (*light candle*). Shine into the dark places and expose the sins of greed, oppression, hate and violence. Fill us with love, joy, peace, patience and a willingness to forgive.

O Christ, you are the light of the world (*light candle*). We pray for the homeless, the refugees, the expelled and forgotten people everywhere. Strengthen us in our belief that you are a God of justice. Empower us with the determination to work for basic human rights.

O Christ, you are the light of the world (*light candle*). We pray for people everywhere and in particular for the people of the Middle East. Show us how we are to live together as neighbours, understanding and respecting one another. We remember before you the many places in the world where there is conflict between nations. We pray that love may determine a just solution.

O Christ, you are the light of the world
(*light candle*). As the Risen Christ you
broke the chains of death; free us from
every kind of oppression. Breathe your
Holy Spirit upon us. Make us a people
of hope, who live in lands where there
is peace and justice for everyone.

Written by women of Jerusalem

God,
bless the peacemakers.
  Bless those who work in home
      and community to end a quarrel,
  bless those who keep faith
      with arguing churches,
  bless those who speak a careful word
      in corridors of power,
  bless those who live good and hopeful
      lives in refugee camps,
  bless those who minister to the military,
  bless those who seek peace with you
      and give your peace away.
Bless all our peacemakers
      with the powerful presence
      and support of your Holy Spirit,
  and the confidence that comes
      through following in the steps
      of Christ.
Amen.

Neil Thorogood

PRAYING FOR JUSTICE

Let justice roll down like waters, and
righteousness like an ever-flowing stream.

Amos 5.24

Our world is so unfair that many of the
injustices that beset our fellow human beings
pass unnoticed. So this section begins with
prayers for forgiveness, and includes prayers
for people we ourselves have treated unfairly,
through discrimination or stigmatization.
And there are prayers that acknowledge the
suffering of whole peoples and nations,
echoing the prophet's call for God's justice
to 'roll down like waters'.

Justice for individuals and communities

A prayer of confession

Loving, life-giving God,
you have spoken to us, and called us
    to be your disciples.
Too often we allow ourselves to be silenced
    by those who are indifferent
    to our insights and our experience.
Forgive us and make us strong
    to raise our voices in hope.

We allow ourselves to be silenced
    by our own fear and self-doubt.
Forgive us and make us strong
    to raise our voices in hope.

We allow ourselves to be silenced
    by the structures of power
    which dominate and determine our lives.
Forgive us and make us strong
    to raise our voices in hope.

By our silence we allow the powers
    of injustice and death to have
    the last word.
**Forgive us and make us strong
    to raise our voices in hope.**

May we be silent no longer,
    but raise our voices to share
    what we have seen and heard.
**It is Christ who meets us,
    calls us by our name,
    and sends us as his apostles.
Amen.**

North London Justice and Peace Network

A prayer for forgiveness

For our incapacity to feel the sufferings
    of others,
and our tendency to live comfortably
    with injustice,
God, forgive us.

For the self-righteousness
    which denies guilt,
and the self-interest
    which strangles compassion,
God, forgive us.

For those who live their lives
    in careless unconcern,
who cry 'Peace, peace'
    when there is no peace,
we ask your mercy.

For our failings in community,
our lack of understanding,
we ask your mercy.

For our lack of forgiveness,
    openness, sensitivity,
God, forgive us.

For the times we were too eager
    to be better than others,
when we are too rushed to care,
when we are too tired to bother,
when we don't really listen,
when we are too quick to act
    from motives other than love,
God, forgive us.

Pietermaritzburg Agency for Christian Social Awareness

A baptism prayer

O God, whose creative spirit
moved over the face of the deep;
who led your people to freedom
through the waters of the exodus;
who promised the poor
that they would never thirst again;
and who ushered us each into life,
breaking the waters of birth;
cherish your world with water
that we may drink and wash and grow;
and bless your *children*
now to be baptized.
As our Saviour Christ
went down into the Jordan
that he might enter our human struggle
and die our death,
so may *they* die with Christ,
and be raised to the new life in him,
as *members* of a worldwide community
that is thirsty for justice,
and longs for your living water.

Christian Aid/Janet Morley

A prayer for those unjustly imprisoned

Almighty Father, you sent your Son to
bring to the whole world the glorious
liberty of the children of God. Open the
eyes of the oppressor and the torturer to
the blindness of their injustice. Open the
way of freedom to those in prison for
what they believe. Anoint us with your
Spirit to make us servants of the oppressed
and instruments of your power, so that
justice and peace may embrace, and your
love may rule in the hearts of all. We ask
this through our Lord Jesus Christ, your
Son, who lives and reigns with you and
the Holy Spirit, one God, for ever
and ever.
Amen.

Amnesty International

A prayer for the homeless

Jesus, as a baby you were a refugee, as a man, you had no place to lay your head. Make us aware of the homeless on our streets and of families without adequate shelter. Give us wisdom to deal with the causes of these problems, that all may work together for better living conditions.

World Day of Prayer

*

Prayers for those who suffer from
the consequences of HIV/AIDS

Jesus, giver of life and hope,
you knew the love of a human family
and the warm companionship
    of your disciples;
and though few of them remained
    with you at Calvary,
you found even there the support
    of your friend and
your mother and of unnamed women.
We pray that those today
    who live with HIV and AIDS
may also be blessed with tender
    and loving companions,
who will give them practical help
    in their times of need
and offer them hope
    in their times of darkness.
May they find in us too
    an unseen source of strength
as they and we are held together
    in your love.
Amen.

Christian Aid/Paula Clifford

Come to us, God of peace.
Come with your reconciling power,
that fear may be cast out by love,
prejudice be replaced by trust,
hostility give way to gentleness.
Come to us, God of peace.

Come to us, God of justice
that we may hear the cries of those oppressed
by AIDS in every land,
calling us, like Jesus the healer,
to walk with them in the search for justice
and mercy.
Come to us, God of justice.

Come to us, God of love.
Come that we may see you in the poor,
    the lonely,
and those who have AIDS.
Come that we might respond to them
    as your compassionate Church.
Come that we may see you
    in people of every race
and commit ourselves to the hope
    that we celebrate
our life together in true community
    and justice.
Come to us, God of love.

Adapted from Dorothy McMahon

Prayers for those who experience
gender discrimination

Mother and Father of all people,
for the women whose gender
    has denied them
promotion or dignity or human rights,
we bring our prayers;
for the women whose gender
    has enabled them
to create, to inspire and to provide,
we bring our praises.

Christian Aid/Peter Graystone

Lord Jesus,
who made time to chat
    with the woman at the well,
who gave the prostitute back her dignity,
who included Mary, Joanna and Suzanna
    among your followers and
who recognized the value
    of the widow's mite,
we pray for women around the world
who have to walk miles to collect water
    because they have no well,
who have no option but to sell their bodies
    to prevent their children going hungry,
who have no acknowledged place in society
    as their opinions don't matter,
who have no access to banks
    because they are too poor
    and insignificant.
Give them time for idle conversation,
    dignity and recognition,
    a voice that is heard
    and make them powerful instruments
    for change.
Amen.

Christian Aid/Eildon Dyer

A prayer for refugees

Lord of the journey,
we ask for your protection on all
    who have fled their homes:
grant them strength on their journeys;
grant that they may find places of
    compassion at which to rest;
ease their fear as they throw in their lot
    with strangers;
and, God of all the world,
    keep alive their vision
of returning to a secure
    and welcoming home.
Amen.

Christian Aid/Peter Graystone

✳

Prayers for those in the fight
against injustice

God of truth,
we pray for all whom you call
to the task of being prophets.

To those crying for justice
in a world controlled by material profit,
Holy God, bring strength and perseverance.

To those imprisoned
for having dared to challenge the powers,
Holy God, bring courage and hope.

To those vilified or misunderstood
for threatening closely-held assumptions,
Holy God, bring wisdom and determination.

To those ridiculed or ignored
for speaking peace in the midst of violence,
Holy God, bring a sense of your kingdom.

And to your Church,
unsure how to speak and be heard,
but struggling to find a prophetic voice,
**Holy God, bring faith
and the confidence that comes
     from confessing Christ as Lord.
Amen.**

Mary Cotes

A Dalit prayer

God of all
It's so hard to live on the margins –
Lonely and forgotten,
Despised ...
Despondent ...
Remember me,
Put back my confidence
Restore my dignity
And walk down the edges with me ...

Then knowing you, Lord,
I shall rise ...
Rise in hope.

Church of South India

A prayer of intercession

Father, as your people suffered long ago
in Egypt and on their journey into
the Promised Land, so your twin peoples,
the Jews and the Palestinians, suffer today.
We pray that current moves down the road
towards peace may be purposeful,
may be supported from all sides, and may
eventually achieve genuine justice and
security for all those on either side
of the current battle lines.
Lord, hear us.
Lord, graciously hear us.

Jesus, who suffered man's inhumanity
to man, we pray for the shattered people
of Africa: people whose poverty is made
worse by their inability to see the fruit
of their labour at a fair price on world
markets, or whose own markets are
flooded with unjustly subsidized goods;
people whose lives are put at risk by killer
diseases such as malaria and tuberculosis,
and who cannot obtain the drugs they need
at prices they can afford; people who die

daily in wars, fed by the arms traders of
wealthy nations. We pray that those with
power over the world's market places may
seek fairness before the so-called freedom
of trade, a freedom that so often benefits
the modern money-changers more than
it services the poor.
Lord, hear us.
Lord, graciously hear us.

Holy Spirit, move over the churches,
causing those who are blind to injustice
and to poverty to look beyond their
rosaries and their altars to the world for
which Christ died. Strengthen those who
so powerfully and sacrificially stand for
the cause of right, and support those quiet
souls who put so much effort into raising
money, both combining to bring about life
before death for people they will never
know, but who they do know are their
brothers and sisters and your children.
Lord, hear us.
Lord, graciously hear us.

Christian Aid/Richard Buckley

Justice in the world

The poor of the world are thirsty
for justice and for peace,
their journey is unending
till hate and oppression cease.

The Lord of Heaven is thirsty
for justice and for peace;
his battle is unending
till hate and oppression cease.

Pastoral Team of Bambamarca

*

I dream of a community
where justice is practised
where human rights are observed,
where racism does not exist
where leaders are honest and able,
where politicians listen in silence.
I dream of a lot more and I still
believe God will provide.

Clementine Naita (adapted)

Lord God, our maker and our redeemer,
this is your world and we are your people:
come among us and save us.

We have wilfully misused your gifts
    of creation;
Lord, be merciful:
forgive us our sin.

We have seen the ill-treatment of others
and have not gone to their aid;
Lord, be merciful:
forgive us our sin.

We have condoned evil and dishonesty
and failed to strive for justice;
Lord, be merciful:
forgive us our sin.

We have heard the good news of Christ,
but have failed to share it with others;
Lord, be merciful:
forgive us our sin.

We have not loved you with all our heart,
nor our neighbours as ourselves;
Lord, be merciful:
forgive us our sin.

New Patterns for Worship

We dare to imagine a world
where hunger has no chance
    to show its face.
We dare to dream of a world
where war and terror are afraid
    to leave their mark.
We long to believe in a world
of hope unchained and lives unfettered.
We dare to share in the creation of a world
where your people break free.

Dare we open our minds to difference?
Dare we open our lives to change?

Your kingdom come, O Lord,
your will be done.
Amen.

Linda Jones

A prayer of invocation

Open our eyes, O God,
    to your worldwide vision.
May we see you at work around the globe
    through the people of God
    committed to reducing injustice.
As your royal priesthood and
        kingdom followers,
    may we be inspired to join in your reign,
the reign begun by Jesus,
    extended by our forebears,
    and continued through us.
Amen.

From Words for Worship

*

God of the hungry, the homeless,
    the helpless,
Make us hunger and thirst
    until their rights prevail.
God of the stateless, the uprooted,
    the refugee,
Make us hunger and thirst
    till their rights prevail.
God of the prisoner, the prophet,
    the protester,
Make us hunger and thirst till your Word,
through them, is heard.
Amen.

Jean Mortimer

Holy God,
if the world insists
    that the weak need the strong,
remind us that in your kingdom
the strong also need the weak.

If the world tells us
    that the fate of the poor
must be dictated by the rich,
remind us that in your kingdom
the rich are transformed by the poor.

If the world declares
    that peace is made by violence,
remind us that in your kingdom
peace joins hands with justice.

If the world believes
    that there is nothing more to hope for,
remind us that your kingdom is built
by those who expect their God to come.
Amen.

Mary Cotes

Three graces

Food three times a day.
Some food every third day.
We live in an unjust world.
As our bodies are nourished,
nourish our anger at injustice, we pray.
Amen.

Ian M. Fraser

*

We have food.
Others are hungry.
May we use the strength
this food gives
to work for justice.

Ruth Burgess

*

O God, to those who have hunger
    give bread,
and to us who have bread
    give the hunger for justice.
Amen.

From Latin America

＊

What do you bring to Christ's table?
We bring bread,
made by many people's work,
from an unjust world
where some have plenty
and most go hungry.

At this table all are fed,
and no one turned away.
Thanks be to God.

What do you bring to Christ's table?
We bring wine,
made by many people's work,
from an unjust world
where some have leisure
and most struggle to survive.

At this table all share the cup
of pain and celebration,
and no one is denied.
Thanks be to God.

These gifts shall be for us
the body and blood of Christ.
Our witness against the hunger,
our cry against injustice,
and our hope for a world
where God is fully known
and every child is fed.
Thanks be to God.

Brian Wren

A collect

Vulnerable God,
You challenge the powers that rule this world
Through the needy, the compassionate
And those who are filled with longing.
Make us hunger and thirst
    to see right prevail,
And single-minded in seeking peace,
That we may see your face
And be satisfied in you,
Through Jesus Christ.
Amen.

Janet Morley

O God, to whom we owe
more than we can count,
in our desire to control
all that will come to be,
we hold your children in the grip of debt
which they cannot repay;
and make them suffer now
the poverty we dread.

Do not hold us to our debts,
but unchain our fear,
that we may release others
into an open future
of unbounded hope
through Jesus Christ our Saviour.
Amen.

Christian Aid/Janet Morley

*

From my wealth and poverty,
I want to live your jubilee.

Help me to give, act and pray
to share your good news:

for the poor –
release from unpayable debt;

for the rich –
freedom from the power of money.

Christian Aid/Rebecca Dudley

Father, your word cries out for justice and
mercy to the poor and oppressed. We have
no strength to speak out, to stand up for
justice to the poor. But you are our strength
and your word is our guide. Help us to do
what is right. Help us to challenge the
structures of today that keep the poor
in bondage to debt, while the rich world
profits. Help us to take action and proclaim
a day of freedom. Have mercy on us, Lord,
and on our nations.
Amen.

From The Debt Cutters Handbook

We dare to pray:
Lord, let the world be changed,
for we long to see the end of poverty;
we dare to pray:
Lord, let the rules be changed,
for we long to see trade
    bring justice to the poor;
we dare to pray:
Lord, let our lives be changed,
for we long to bring hope
    where good news is needed.
In the strength of your Spirit,
and inspired by your compassion,
we make this promise to work for change,
and wait confidently for the day
when you make all things new.

Christian Aid/ Peter Graystone

*

Our hands are not machines
in the factories of profit,
our bodies are not just robots
for production of wealth.

Our lives are given dignity
by God
not by possessions.
Our dreams achieve their
quality in freedom
not control.

Our job is joy,
our labour creation,
our business peace,
our task to be.
Be with us, Lord, in rest and work.
Our hope is to live life
and live it to the full.

CAFOD/Linda Jones

God of the just weight
and the fair measure,
let me remember the hands
that harvested my food, my drink,
not only in my prayers
but on the marketplace.
Let me not seek a bargain
that leaves others hungry.

Christian Aid/Janet Morley

❋

Tilt the scales,
O God of the mustard seed:
That the poor shall see justice.

Share the feast,
O God of Eden's abundant garden:
That each crop may fetch a fair price.

Upset the tables,
O God of the upside-down Kingdom:
That the least can benefit from their trade.

Open our eyes,
O God of life in all its fullness:
That we may learn to walk
the way of your son
tilting, sharing, upsetting this world

Not satisfied
until the products we bring to our table
Give a better deal,
to all who hunger for one.

In His name,
Amen.

Christian Aid/Simeon Mitchell

God, thank you for:

fresh herbs and
exotic spices

local produce and
tropical fruit

for the bounty and gifts of your good earth.

May we remember all who work the land.
May our choices and actions
    be seeds that grow
to yield our brothers and sisters
    a rich harvest
of healthier working conditions,
    living wages,
a fair trade ...
Amen.

Neil Paynter

✳

Angry Jesus,
as of old you entered
     into that temple market
casting out the merchants
     and money changers;
enter now into the markets
     of our modern world.
Throw out of them all that is unworthy,
     unjust and self-seeking
and direct the market forces of the world
in the ways of justice, plenty and peace,
for your tender mercy's sake.
Amen.

Christian Aid

Praying for lawmakers

A prayer for governments

O Lord, our God,
    we pray for the governments
        and rulers of the nations.
Do not permit them to shed innocent blood,
    but inspire them to rule
        according to your will
        as you intend for them to do.
May they promote the good
        and repress the evil,
    so that we who fear your name
    may lead quiet and peaceful lives
        here on earth.
Give leaders the spirit of wisdom and justice.
Let all who exercise authority
    remember that they have over them
        a God in heaven;
Let them not pervert power
    which you have delegated unto them,
    and may they be a blessing to the nation.
May we respect and obey the laws
        that right and good may be promoted.
Let us live peaceably with each other,
    respecting one another,
        and serving God faithfully and in love.
Amen.

From Words for Worship

The prayer of the House of Commons

Almighty God, by whom alone kings reign and princes decree justice, and from whom alone cometh all counsel, wisdom, and understanding,

We, thine unworthy servants, here gathered together in thy name, do most humbly beseech thee to send down the heavenly wisdom from above, to direct and guide us in all our consultations:

And grant that, we having thy fear always before our eyes, and laying aside all private interests, prejudices, and partial affections, the result of all our counsels may be the glory of thy blessed name, the maintenance of true religion and justice, and the safety, honour and happiness of the *King*, the public welfare, peace and tranquillity of the realm, and the uniting and knitting together of the hearts of all persons and estates towards one another,

Through Jesus Christ our Lord and Saviour.

Sir Christopher Yelverton, MP for Northampton and
Speaker of the House, c.1578

A prayer for the United Nations

O God, by whose power alone men and women are enabled to live together as brothers and sisters, give wisdom and understanding to all who work through the United Nations for peace and justice among the nations, and grant them such a sense of unity and purpose in their common task that they may build a world of righteousness and peace, through Jesus Christ our Lord, **Amen.**

From Prayers for Peacemakers

CHRIST OUR PEACE

Jesus said, 'Abide in me as I abide in you.'
John 15.4

At the beginning of his ministry Jesus
announced that he had come to bring good
news to the poor. And before he died he
promised that those who love him would
know his abiding presence with them.
The concluding prayers celebrate these two
aspects of the gospel message and ask that
Christ's blessing may be on us as we seek
his peace and justice for ourselves.

✳

A prayer of petition

Show us, Good Lord,
how to be frugal, till all are fed;
how to weep, till all can laugh;
how to be meek, till all can stand in pride;
how to mourn, till all are comforted;
how to be restless, till all live in peace;
how to claim less, till all find justice.
Amen.

Peter Millar

A statement of commitment

I do not choose wealth;
I do not choose poverty –
I choose liberty.
I do not choose merriment;
I do not choose misery –
I choose life.
I do not choose success;
I do not choose failure –
I choose Jesus.

Christian Aid/Peter Graystone

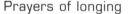

Prayers of longing

Creator God,
give us a heart for simple things:
    love and laughter
    bread and wine
    tales and dreams.
Fill our lives
with green and growing hope;
make us a people of justice
whose song is Alleluia
and whose name breathes love.

A prayer from Africa

We want to celebrate life!
We cry out against all that kills life:
hunger, poverty, unemployment, sickness,
repression, individualism, injustice.
We want to announce fullness of life:
work, education, health, housing,
     bread for all.
We want communion,
a world renewed;
we hope against hope.
With the Lord of history,
we want to make all things new.

A group of Brazilian young people

*

Give us, Lord God, a vision of our world
    as your love would make it:
a world where the weak are protected,
    and none go hungry or poor;
a world where the benefits of civilized
    life are shared, and everyone
    can enjoy them;
a world where different races, nations
    and cultures live in tolerance
    and mutual respect;
a world where peace is built with justice,
    and justice is guided by love;
and give us the inspiration
    and courage to build it,
        through Jesus Christ our Lord.
Amen.

Author unknown

❋

O God of many names
Lover of all nations
We pray for peace

In our hearts
In our homes
In our nations
In our world

The peace of your will
The peace of our need.

George Appleton

✳

Come to the living God,
   Come to stand alongside the poor.
   Come to struggle with those
      who seek freedom.
   Come to resist all that offends
      God's justice.
Come to the living, disturbing God.

Jan Berry

An offertory prayer

God of extravagant mercy,
   with hands outstretched
     you have poured out
     wonder and pleasure and delight,
     goodness and beauty and bounty.
So take these offerings, we pray,
     as our protest against all
     that is evil and ugly and impoverished,
     trivial and wretched and tyrannical,
     in our world and ourselves –
And thus may we and others
     know ourselves to be blessed.
Amen.

Terry Falls and Beryl Turner

Blessings

May the blessing of God go before you.
May her grace and peace abound.
May her spirit live within you.
May her love wrap you round.
May her blessing remain with you always.
May you walk on holy ground.
Amen.

Celebrating Women, No. 155

May the God
   who binds up the brokenhearted,
who proclaims freedom
to those held captive by poverty,
and promises
to all who mourn its loss,
bless you with beauty instead of ashes,
the oil of gladness in place of grief,
and instead of your spirit of despair,
a garment of unending praise;
through Jesus Christ our Lord,
Amen.

Christian Aid

May the Lord God lead us from this place
and take us to where he is living;
May he lead us to a new awareness
    of the poor
and show us his home among them;
May he lead us to a new desire for justice
and give us a glimpse of the Kingdom
    he is building;
May he fill our hearts with generosity
and anoint us to be bearers of good news;
May his blessing be upon us
    as it is upon the poor,
And may he show us what he wants us to do.
Amen.

Christian Aid

May the blessing of the God
    of peace and justice be with us;
May the blessing of the Son
    who weeps the tears
    of the world's suffering be with us;
And may the blessing of the Spirit
    who inspires us to reconciliation
    and hope be with us;
from now into eternity.
Amen.

Clare McBeath

INDEX OF FIRST LINES

INDEX OF AUTHORS AND SOURCES

ACKNOWLEDGEMENTS

The compilers and publisher gratefully acknowledge
permission to reproduce copyright material in this
anthology. Every effort has been made to trace
and contact copyri0ght holders. If there are any
inadvertent omissions we apologize to those
concerned and will ensure that a suitable
acknowledgement is made at the next reprint.

Abingdon Press: Adapted from Walter Russell Bowie,
Lift up your hearts, 1956, by permission (p. 15).
The Archbishops' Council: *Common Worship:
Services and Prayers for the Church of England*,
2000; *The Alternative Service Book 1980*; *New
Patterns for Worship*, 2002 (pp. 26, 44, 74).
Ateliers et Presses de Taizé, 71250 Taizé Community,
France ©: Prayer by Brother Roger of Taizé 10 (p. 19).
Brethren Press 1451 Dundee Avenue, Elgin, Illinois:
Kenneth L. Gibble, *For All Who Minister*, copyright
1993, by permission (p. 12).
British Council of Churches: Rubem Alves, *All Year
Round* (p. 13).
CAFOD: Linda Jones (p. 79).
The Canterbury Press Norwich © Peter W Millar
An Iona Prayer Book, 1998, by permission (p. 87).
The Canterbury Press: copyright Neil Thorogood,
'Bless the Peacemakers' in *Timeless Prayers for Peace*
compiled by Geoffrey Duncan 2002 (p. 48).
The Canterbury Press: The Church of South India
in, *Timeless Prayers for Peace* compiled by Geoffrey
Duncan, 2002 (p. 63).

Christian Aid (p. 57).

Christian Aid, Janet Morley *Life before death, An Anthology for Christian Aid Week*, 1991 (p. 54).

Christian Aid, on their 50th birthday, 1995 (p. 7).

Christian Aid/Jubilee 2000 Committee, Adapted by R. Dudley for *Breaking the Chains*, from Julia Esquivel, *Those who saw the star: A poem on the Incarnation, Confessing our faith around the world: The Caribbean and Central America*, WCC, 1985 (p. 6).

Christian Aid/Jubilee 2000: *Ideas for a service: Third World Debt* (p. 83).

Christian Aid: *A full measure, overflowing* (p. 94).

Christian Aid: Eildon Dyer (p. 60).

Christian Aid: *Feast for Life, Christian Aid's material for Harvest 1995* (p. 93).

Christian Aid: Honduras (p. 80).

Christian Aid: Janet Morley (p. 76).

Christian Aid: Peter Graystone (pp. 35, 40, 45, 59, 61, 78, 85).

Christian Aid: Rebecca Dudley (p. 77).

Christian Aid: Richard Buckley (p. 64).

Christian Conference of Asia Youth: Alison O'Grady (ed.), *Your Will Be Done*, September 1984, October 1986 (p. 42).

Corrymeela Community, Ireland (p. 32).

The Corrymeela Press: *Celebrating Together: Prayers, Liturgies and Songs from Corrymeela* (1987) (p. 90).

Crossroad/Herder & Herder: Miriam T. Winter, *Woman Word: A Feminist Lectionary and Psalter: Women of the New Testament*, adapted, 1990 (p. 33).

Desclée de Brouwer: Dom Helder Camara, *The Desert is Fertile*, Orbis Books, 1974. Originally

published in French as *Le Desert est Fertile*, Desclée
de Brouwer. Reprinted by permission of Georges
Borchardt, Inc., for Desclée de Brouwer copyright
© 1974 (p. 20).

Fairtrade Fortnight: Simeon Mitchell, 2001 (p. 81).

The Hengrave Community Prayer (p. 43).

Herald Press Scottdale, PA 15683: Arlene M. Mark
(ed.), *Words for Worship*, All rights reserved (pp. 17,
21, 22, 34, 39, 69, 84).

IBRA: Christian Education: Jean Mortimer,
reproduced from Maureen Edwards (ed.), *Words
for Today*, 1998, with the permission of Christian
Education (p. 70).

Jubilee 2000: *The Debt Cutters Handbook* (p. 77).

Medical Mission Sisters: *Celebrating Women* No. 155,
'May the blessing of God go before you' © 1987
(p. 93).

A Palestinian Christian, Christian Aid (p. 36).

Palestinian women, Jerusalem (p. 45).

Pastor Kameeta from Namibia (p. 3).

The Pilgrim Press: Ruth C. Duck, *Hear the
invitation of the prophet Isaiah* in *Touch Holiness:
Resources for Worship*, ed. Ruth C. Duck and
Maren C. Tirabassi, copyright © 1990, by permission
(p. 2).

A poor community in Central America (p. 8).

Roots Worship Issue 10 © Clare McBeath (pp. 9, 94).

Roots Worship: Linda Jones 20.10.02 (p. 68).

SCM Press: A short extract from Pastoral Team
of Bambamarca, *Vamos Caminando: A Peruvian
Catechism*, 1985 (p. 66).

SCM Press: Caryl Micklem (ed.), *Contemporary
Prayers for Church and School*, © 1975, by
permission (p. 31).

Sir Christopher Yelverton, MP for Northampton and
Speaker of the House, circa 1578 (p. 85).

SPCK Triangle: Babylonian Talmud, *Praying with the
Jewish Tradition*, Paula Clifford, 1988, by permission
(p. 25).

SPCK Triangle: St. Augustine, *Confessions XIII,
Praying with St. Augustine*, 1987, by permission
(p. 19).

SPCK: Alan Paton, *Prayers Encircling the World*,
1998, by permission (p. 29).

SPCK: Janet Morley, *All Desires Known*, 1992 (p. 75).

SPCK: Pietermaritzburg Agency for Christian Social
Awareness, South Africa, Janet Morley (ed.) *Bread
of Tomorrow*, 1992 (p. 52).

WCC: A group of Brazilian young people, in *With all
God's People*, 1989 (p. 89).

Terry Waite (p. 28).

Wild Goose Publications: A Fair Trade © Neil
Paynter, from *Blessed be our table: Graces for
mealtimes and reflections on food*, 2003 (p. 82).

Wild Goose Publications: 'To work for justice'
© Ruth Burgess, from *Blessed be our table: Graces
for mealtimes and reflections on food*, 2003 (p. 72).

Wild Goose: 'Nourish our anger' © Ian Fraser from
*Blessed be our table: Graces for mealtimes and
reflections on food*, 2003 (p. 72).

Women's World Day of Prayer, 1990 (p. 14).

World Council of Churches Ecumenical Women's
Solidarity Fund: Carolyn Boyd, Programme
Co-ordinator, Croatia/Bosnia (p. 38).